Opening Words

Why Social Media and Business Intelligence?

Social media and Business Intelligence are now inseparable. Even the most basic user of any social media service asks himself such questions as "How many followers do I have?", "What's trending today?", "How do people feel about...?"

It is the job of Business Intelligence to tease out these answers in a comprehensive and scientific way so that the information can be organized and stored in a way that provides business value. This allows for companies to gain competitive edge, cut costs and release products with a higher degree of success.

Combining social media and business intelligence for small and medium sized enterprises is even more crucial. It allows them a greater audience reach, more effective targeting and greater cost savings. Advertising and marketing campaigns can be created more efficiently.

Maturity

The market for these tools is now very mature. All of the top technology vendors, from IBM to Oracle and Microsoft are fully committed to maintaining a permanent presence in the Social Media and Business Intelligence space. Information on consumer trends, pricing, sentiment and requirements are now available directly from the consumer and do not require outsourcing to third party surveys or last years data. The content that comes from social media and feeds the business intelligence systems is created and analyzed in real time.

Cost & variety

Today there is a wide variety of products and services available to serve a wide spectrum of budgets and levels of technical expertise. Some companies may require deep analysis of big data, while others merely need to check in on Facebook statistics. Developing your SMBI (Social Media/Business Intelligence) strategy requires you to evaluate your budget, requirements and technical abilities.

User Friendly

Gaining business insight from social media interaction data is no longer a matter of hiring a database administrator to churn out reports, hoping that he understands the business points you are trying to uncover. Today, most SMBI tools allow a business oriented end user access to the user friendly dashboard that provides a wide variety of views and perspectives on real time data.

Integration

Because these tools are now so user friendly, they have now permeated throughout the entire business structure and are informing the internal business processes of many organizations. Real time social media analysis doesn't just define what products to make, it also defines how those products are made. It doesn't just facilitate customer relations, it defines them. Companies that can effectively tap into customer requirements along with market trends will be best positioned to succeed.

The Time is Now

Two years ago one could be forgiven, perhaps, for seeing marketing via Facebook and Twitter as a trend that would soon be replaced by another technology trend, the same way that Second Life seemed to have fallen off the map. This technology trend does not rely on Twitter and Facebook, however.

Take those two web sites out of the equation and the phenomena of social media will still be present and continually evolving. The issue isn't a particular web service, its an overall redesign of communications technology. This new technology creates and makes available massive amounts of communications, relationships, sentiments, trends and demographic data. This data is now presented in easily readable format and made freely available via a huge set of tools.

In the same way that traditional businesses could not succeed without marketing, a business today cannot succeed without using the powerful insights that social media and business intelligence provide.

Without the combination of Social Media and Business Intelligence, business today is simply not possible.

Preface: Social Media and Business Intelligence

Social Media is already very well known and widely used, but there is still a great deal of misunderstanding as to how it can be used effectively by business organizations. There are many claims that social media is essential to business, but understanding the hard science behind how this relatively new technology can create solid ROI can be confusing.

In this textbook you will cover the relationship between all the useful data that social media generates and a companies marketing, product creation, CRM and business processes.

It covers the current state of mature technologies and methods for getting the most out of social media data by using analytics and business intelligence.

This paper is provided by CIOWhitePapers, a leading source of technical white papers by industry experts such as Oracle, IBM, Google, Forrester Consulting, Wildfire, Hootsuite and a wide variety of drivers in the Emerging Marketing and IT sector.

CIOWhitePapers also publishes a free companion to this paper, '100 pages, 100 Tips – The Definitive Social Media Strategy Kit'. It is a comprehensive set of rules that industry leaders follow when running their own successful social media marketing campaigns. It provides details on how to run a campaign and get the most out of the business intelligence a well monitored effort can provide.

100 Pages, 100 Tips, Definitive Social Media Strategy Kit

1 Introduction

Since 2010, when Social Media first became an internet buzzword, it has proven itself to be not only a cultural facilitator, but also a very real business tool. Social networks powerfully differentiate themselves from previous internet marketing channels in that on a daily basis, they are gathering, parsing and sorting the commercially valuable demographic data of the end user.

Social Media now describes wide range of services, communications and evolutions that are concurrently taking place throughout cyberspace. While the phrase is descriptive, it is better to think of it as one of many views of the internet. It is important to recognize social media as a subset of a larger whole where the component parts and various platforms, protocols and devices are all different ways to see the same distributed information, communications and manufacturing networks.

What has generated a lot of the attention on the phrase social media is its potential to bring larger customer bases to smaller organizations that produce for increasingly niche markets, to make target customer metrics more granular and to enable the empowerment of the end user and client, giving them a sense of governance over how the products that serve them are created.

This is because social networks bring the following functionality to the table:

Collection of user demographic data.

As social networks and internet applications grow more complex, extended and more niche specific data is now being accumulated and distributed to companies who use this data to learn more about their customers and create more effective, timely and authentic promotions.

The ability of user<->user interactions to create evangelistic communities.

Face to face promotion of a product from satisfied customer to potential customer is some of the most effective marketing available today. At the same time it also provides a reliable source of research for people considering a particular purchase. When amplified by the scope and processing speed of the internet, it is an extremely powerful form of promotion.

Companies are fooling themselves if they think that they can continue with traditional media alone. The potential benefits of initiating an evangelical wave are enormous in terms of generating loyalty, audience reach and sales. The trick and area of development that needs to be mastered is how to generate these waves in such a way that is reliable and measurable.

The fact that as a socially interactive medium, the internet serves as a powerful link between internal corporate processes and the client/consumer who is also the end user of a social network.

The appearance of this pathway between functions in the business cycle is just beginning to define itself, but it is already clear that there are a few gaps that will result in extensive opportunities for companies that can facilitate efficient flow and interpretation of data along these roads while demonstrating tangible, not ethereal, ROI.

The pulse of ongoing dialog within Social networks/media can be tapped to reveal community and consumer sentiment to a degree that traditional poll/focus group measurements cannot, particularly with regards to authenticity, the proximity to how a client or customer feels outside of a controlled environment. In addition, this consumer feedback is digitally inputted and easily parseable in a way that is suitable for Business Intelligence and operations processes to consume and turn into ongoing optimization.

Of course, there is a lot of hype about social media, and this overabundance of exuberance has resulted in many people overlooking the actual tangible benefits of the phenomenon in terms of its ability to, at the end of the day, make more money. Social media by itself, does not generate cash. This has probably been overstated by now to the point that the internet consulting space is overflowing with people practically advertising their ability to not make money on the web, as though this is an unproductive behavior.

They instead talk about social capital, social authority, mind share and all manner of methods to gain high social ranking, it is social media after all. Social Media is no longer a buzzword for slick marketing gurus, it is a real group of technologies that enable businesses to make more money. It fits into the business cycle between product creation, business strategy, public relations, marketing and business intelligence. The appearance of a social internet has revealed a path between all of these previously disparate areas. While one or two have been connected before, today the development of a pathways between all of them is now plausible.

The technology gaps that existed in 2010 have been rapidly filled by various companies and organizations. They are using new applications and methods to create a more compelling value proposition to their existing and potential customers. Companies that are top in their industries are now create efficiencies and gain valuable real time insight that allows them to be more flexible and agile in serving their base. This opportunity has been particularly kind to small and medium sized businesses, who have been able to rapidly gain new customers that had previously been very difficult to find.

Social Media creates a unique set of links in a chain that connect customers to the companies that serve them. Each link provides large amounts of data that in turn allows companies of all sizes to gain massive competitive edge.

In this white paper we'll take a look at the various components of this chain, as well as the areas that need further development in order for companies of all kinds to either contribute to or benefit from this technological evolution.

2   What is 'Out' in Social Media and what is 'In'

First, let's take a look at what has gone out since 2010 and what has gained traction and shown real ROI.

Out	In
The Social Media Guru: The guy who has all kinds of 'soft' communication strategies and is an expert in creating a twitter account. A short lived phase during which people with a sales background attempted to ride the hype into big money. They had little technical expertise.	Social Media Analytics, Business Intelligence. With data now largely available via APIs and various analytics services. The job is to form an engaging content strategy and monitor interaction with it.
Web Tools to Broadcast to Multiple Social Media Sites. (ping.fm) Useful for a time, but many of the sites now offer cross platform publishing. There are plugins on Facebook, for example, which allow for posting to Twitter.	Broadcasting Coupled with Analytics This has caused sites like ping.fm to differentiate themselves by adding analytics to their product offerings. By teeming up with seesmic, they have done just that.
Web Analytics While web analytics are still in use, they do not provide information on the sentiments and opinions of the sites visitors.	Social Media Analytics Social Media analytics parses through comments related to your brand and products to find out not only opinions, but trends. This also includes competitor insight.
A million Social Media Sites The social media space was once quite a bit more diverse. The fact is, however, a successful site is not determined by the technology, but the users. Even though Twitter suffered through daily crashes and slowdowns, it's loyal user base was impossible to beat.	Youtube, Twitter, LinkedIn, Facebook Following the shakeout, the sites above are the ones with the most engaged and contributing audiences.

Out	In
Spamming, Massive Followers (Quantity)	Targeted Followers
The early days of Facebook and Twitter saw people taking great pride in having many followers. Sending out high volumes of messages was also common.	Since then, marketers have learned to acquire interest by creating content that keeps people interested. They have also learned to target the people they friend more intelligently.
Public Image	Content
With access to such large amounts of data and content, people are now more interested in in-depth material than image.	People are now empowered to seek out and expect more comprehensive material.
The quick sell, impulse buying	Nurturing and Engagement
'Buy now while supplies last' doesn't work online. It is easy to go to google and find a similar product from a competitor.	Consumers expect to be engaged, entertained and nurtured into purchasing. They also expect to become part of a products community, not just customers.
Confused, unmanageable data	Big data
Data was once in a variety of formats with poorly implemented methods of access.	Today, that same data is formatted and configured for delivery via a wide variety of programming interfaces. There are also many tools to convert from one data format and presentation type to another.

3 The 5 Pillars Of Social Media and Business Intelligence

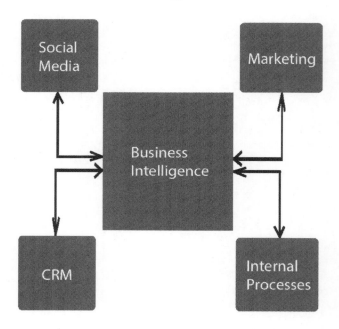

Definition: Social Media Management Systems are a group of applications or methods used to manage and track work flow in a distributed social media environment. They can be manual or automated and enable the manager to listen, aggregate, publish, and manage multiple social media channels from one tool.

How it works: In the most basic sense, there are three simple features:

1) Connect with social media channels.
2) Allow the manager to quickly publish from one location to each of those channels, some provide ability to customize to each channel as well as schedule all or certain messages.
3) Aggregate and Manage social data. The system allows the manager to see an aggregated view of what's happening (from views to comments) and will offer some form of analytics and conversion metrics to varying levels of depth and complexity.

Each of these basic functions can be expanded upon to incredible levels of detail. Social media as a platform has proven itself and is now a part of any marketing mix. At the same time, marketing has come to incorporate many of the features of business intelligence and in many cases connected to internal business processes.

This means that many marketing efforts are created in such a way as to be able to track user reactions in real-time.

Overall, this development has been concurrent and convergent. That is, all these technologies have been evolving on their own unique paths for the last few years while at the same time looking across the bow at other parallel fields of development then converging with them to the extent that they provide value. There is now a great degree of inter-relatedness and it is up to the organization to decide which mix is appropriate to their business.

Those components are:

Social media

Marketing Strategy

Business Intelligence

CRM – managing and nurturing a company's interactions with clients and sales prospects

Internal Business Processes

Each of these components relates to one or more of the others in a functional way that, if done correctly, adds value and efficiencies to to company, its products/services and operations. Let's quickly define each of these terms in order to be clear and also to see how they are different from each other.

Social Media –

This is how individuals and companies use websites who's primary source of content is the end user. Because of this, gaining credibility is a matter of supplying not only good content, but good social interaction. It is, after all, social media. A common starting mistake is to view social media as a platform for email blasts and 'campaigns' rather than as a process of communication. Social Media is not an advanced form of email, it is something else entirely.

While it is certainly possible to attend to customer needs and issues via social media, it is not wise to do so. The data interactions and access rights are all determined by the host of the service, not by you. Social media should be considered more of a broadcast and participation, and even lead generation media.

Social Media relates to other business components in that it informs them with a real time immediacy that has been previously unavailable. This has huge potential for a new set of marketing metrics, The internet is now brimming with companies willing to parse through, store and interpret your social media interactions. Each of them with a different level of granularity, reliability and cost.

The Top Social Media Sites as of 2012 in Terms of Business Analytics:

Site	Strengths	Weaknesses
Facebook	By far, the biggest user base. Powerful API allows for understanding user sentiment and demographics.	Unlike a search engine, users don't come here with a purchase mindset. Ad revenues and stock price reflect this.
Twitter	Short simple messages allow for a large number of data points. Strong, loyal and active community. Many 3rd party apps.	Though more easily readable, short messages contain less data.
Youtube	Biggest video site by far. Powerful API can reveal user trends.	Used less as a communication platform than Twitter or Facebook. Comments on a video tend to be less conversational.
Pinterest	Visually attractive. Loyal users. Large amount of content.	Majority of content is pictures. Comments relate to those pictures. Thus more difficult to determine context.
Meetup	Focused on creating and scheduling meetups coupled with the API, one can locate trends in a geographic area.	Smaller user base.
Tagged	Similar to Facebook.	Much smaller user base
Google +	Advanced technologies, integrated into its email platform. Loyal knowledgeable people.	Less teen and young adult oriented. Growing slowly.
Tumblr	Great for following trends among bloggers. Can give great insight into trend setters.	Smaller user base. Less appealing than Twitter or Facebook for direct promotion. Long term planning required.
LinkedIn	Professional network. Ideal for determining industry trends.	Limits on access, how many people one can follow. More exclusive behavior in general.
Ning	Great for a quick set up of a social website. Includes all of the tools, including analytics.	Ning now costs money. This means a smaller user base. That having been said the users will be more active and provide more data.

CRM –

CRM focuses on service, retention, sales and lead generation. This is the component that addresses the customer on a more one to one level and speaks more specifically on customer related issues such as terms of service, pricing, email lists and the actual sale.

It differs from the social media component in that it is less promotional and participatory and more actionable. It is the mechanism through which deals are closed and customers receive hard goods. Social media informs CRM as to what actions need to be taken and CRM uses social media as a way to broadcast participation and messages that pertain to both current and potential customers. By making social media a CRM component, potential customers can have a first hand look at the company they will be dealing with should they decide to make a purchase.

3.1   Top CRM Vendors 2012 (via CIO Magazine):

SAP

Oracle

Salesforce.com

Cegidim

Amdocs

Aspect

Verint

Microsoft

SAS

Avaya

Marketing strategy –

The methods and tactics used to gain the attention that leads to sales. Both social media and CRM efforts need to rely on a comprehensive approach to the customer that is built on the companies mission statement and long term goals. Without this, the flood of information from a constant stream of services coming online will overwhelm the marketing approach and reduce it to little more than a scramble to answer everyone, one-to-one, in real time.

Marketing to an audience that has this one-to-one potential does not obligate you to speak to everyone. Having these tools requires you to 'choose your battles' for maximum return. In the same way that a short tempered employee can embarrass his whole organization with one rude tweet, a well trained staff can create large positive waves of good will simply by focusing attention on a situation and audience that has high and positive visibility. Locating these spots on the web, these communities and times of day is the function of marketing strategy. Both social media and CRM interactions help to inform this.

3.2   Biggest Companies in Marketing Management and Automation:

Marketo

HootSuite

Eloqua

Radian6

Seesmic

Vitrue

Adobe SocialAnalytics

Silverpop

Pardot

Vocus

Alterian

IBM Unica

Aprimo

Business Intelligence –

The ability to dig into data that has been acquired through disparate channels and business activities and then identify trends, opportunities and areas where efficiency can be improved. As stated above, social media and CRM are used to inform the long term marketing strategy. The problem is the huge volume of data coming from both channels. This is where business intelligence comes in. BI compiles, parses and interprets this data into reports and forms that are consumable by marketers and strategists.

What business intelligence cannot do is change the quality of the data coming in. There does need to be a starting point so that an organization feels comfortable that incoming information is useable by the company, that it comes from the target audience. Locating these sources of useful data is one of the services offered by various consulting companies or dedicated marketing staff. In addition, effective business intelligence requires a staff or consultant who knows what to look for and how to find it, a person who knows how to read data in a way that provides business value.

The majority of social media marketing and enterprise marketing companies providing service today are in this space. That is, collecting data from your interactions and then interpreting it. They either do this for you, provide tools to that end or, as consultants, provide the strategy, recommendations and support for you to implement. Such companies define themselves, and their cost structure based on how comprehensive the data collection is as well as how deep the data analysis goes. Because this is an evolving area, there are many companies that struggle to define what it is that they do and how to integrate their offerings into your business process.

Simple free services count how many Twitter followers you have or how many times someone mentions your name, leaving it up to you to interpret the data. Other companies collect data from Twitter, Facebook and Youtube (Or another collection of sites) and provide some interpretation for a monthly fee. Still other companies do above, with a more robust database implementation a deeper view, plus historical analysis Finally, companies like SAP, Oracle and IBM provide the means to process huge amounts of information and highly complex analysis.

At the low end, there is no marketing and branding consulting included. At the middle tier, such consulting is offered for additional cost and beyond this, various companies are balanced in different ways. Some are more focused on the technology and some are more focused on the branding/marketing/public relations aspect. At the high end, it is assumed that you are paying big bucks for a high end technology solution and that you can accept the cost or have your own resources to handle marketing communication separately.

3.3   Top Business Intelligence Products:

SAP Business Objects

IBM Cognos

SAS

MicroStrategy

Webfocus

SAP Netweaver

Oracle Hyperion

Microsoft Business Intelligence

Internal Business Process and Strategy –

How the company, organization, blogger operates day to day in order to reach targets. Internal processes can be informed by Business intelligence.

What a company does on any given day is a combination of its long term strategy mixed in with the feedback it gets from competitors, customers and industry dynamics. Information from each of these can be had from online activity, research and dialogs. Like marketing strategy, Internal processes don't communicate directly with the end user, they act on data compiled from business intelligence.

There is another sector of social media that connects staff in large company's in their own closed social media network, which can then be tied to outside communication channels, but it is still effectively an internal communication process.

All five parts are represented by the drawing above. Business Intelligence is fed by the other four components. These components connect to Business Intelligence via communication channels that connect internal activity with outward facing activity. The dynamic of all this information broadcasting, collecting interpretation and adjustment is what drives your business, forward. Failure of any component leads to stagnation, a breakdown in business intelligence leads to stagnation causing it to get passed by businesses. Ineffective or unbalanced components will create a business that is out of balance and will eventually suffer failures causing it to go in unproductive circles.

What you pay for when you pay for any of these services is a faster, better running and more efficient organization. You can buy a complete solution or your can assemble your own, the choice is yours.

If you buy a complete solution, with the best components and business intelligence, you'll pay a lot of money. You can assemble a best-of-breed solution, save some money and do the basic assembly yourself You can build your own from scratch, save much more money and have a very flexible and modifiable solution, but you'll need top of the line engineers to build and maintain it for you. If you can do this, you'll then likely have a platform that can be resold to other people, and this is precisely what many companies do, they offer their own framework, one that has worked for them, to other customers.

Having this understanding, you now have to evaluate your needs and match them to your skills and budget. You may want to just jump right in, get a pre-fabricated basic solution and start doing business, but there could be some issues here:

Support issues

Your dependency on the service provider

How easily data can be ported to another system.

The number of options out there is amazing. Here are some examples:

The business intelligence unit goes from the basic, a very low cost Mysql database that you will have to do the scripting on to get the reports out of.

Various single business components that offer the marketing, internal process consulting, business strategy or social media consulting individually. You assemble them together. Various combinations of these components. Here are some examples:

Marketing plus social media

Social media and CRM linkage

Business strategy and marketing communication

Business intelligence connecting one or all of the tires

Internal processes with business intelligence

Theoretically, with 5 parts there should be be 5*4*3*2*1 possibilities resulting in at least one company for each combination of collection of combinations. Obviously, the comprehensiveness and quality of the solutions will drive the costs that a given service provider quotes you, but at least now you have a picture of the myriad choices that face you, both as a customer and as a potential service provider.

Given the above, you most definitely see that knowing your needs and objectives, while it has always been critical, is now even more essential. There is simply too much to choose from for meandering experimentation to be a possibility and these tools really are necessary.

For each mix, there is likely now a company that specializes in that blend. Because given blends are more suited to specific industries, some companies will feel comfortable serving clients in a given industry, as opposed to a particular kind of product. This depends on the scope of the service provider along with how successful they are in retaining business for their defined niche.

4 The 7 Key Reasons You Need Social Media And Enterprise Marketing

Today, Social media is part of the business ecosystem, not separate or autonomous. The question is less of implementation and has more to do with integration into existing business processes. Beyond that, it has the power to change business in fundamental ways. It is this last point that leads many to think that social media is

New

Its own autonomous entity.

First of all, social media is simply the current iteration of the Internet, with user generated content, semantic storage, APIs and far improved parseability via XML/JSON and the community of users as an asset.

Social Media allows a new cultural infrastructure that is more responsive to current and potential customer behaviors. Because this new social internet is becoming so interlinked with the business process, a better term is Enterprise Social Marketing.

Enterprise Social Marketing technologies have rapidly matured and can provide significant value, efficiencies and insight. More compelling is that these tools are giving competitors a cost, authenticity and reach advantage. To be clear, though, let's list the reasons you need to implement an Enterprise Social Marketing solution.

Cost/The Recession –

This recession has been, and still is, so deep that fundamental changes in business thinking will have to occur. This would seemingly not affect an unrelated IT industry, but the devastation wrought by overvaluation has changed business thinking in general to the point that sexy is being replaced with ROI and Real Intrinsic Value.

Customers and clients of all kinds will ask about ROI and less about design, UI and innovation. Markets, businesses and buyers are going right back to basic principles and they need to save money. It's not just a tighten the belt game though, it's business and in business one must still compete, innovate productively, create efficiencies and inspire.

Enterprise marketing and its social media tools have the ability to accomplish these tasks for less money if implemented correctly, and there will be some companies that do. Other organizations will become lost in the myriad choices on offer today (and the myriad more to come), get confused and waste their hard to earn cash. The efficiencies created by integrated marketing with social media are real, as are the risks. Because some of your competitors will get it right and save money that can be used to develop their brand, products and businesses, you also have no choice but to begin defining your approach. If you don't, they'll bury you in cost savings alone, much less the other benefits described below.

Flexibility –

Unlike traditional media, Internet marketing possesses a wide variety of channels to utilize. Video, Banner ads, Injection into communities, Bulletin boards and many others. Every year a new platform and method to advertise on that platform is created. If done correctly, customer engagement can also lead to sales, if not too obvious.

Analytics –

Rather than simply tracking changes in sales after a given campaign, marketers can track activity by site, channel, media, method, message and a wide variety of other metrics. Coupled with real time response capabilities, marketing efforts can adapt and profit from knowledge much faster than before.

Targeting –

Platforms like Facebook allow ad targeting to occur by age, sex, education, location and a whole host of other demographics. There is simply no way that traditional media can accomplish this and even if it could, the cost would be enormous. Online, this cost is much less and direct to the people who's attention you need. Beyond that, public reaction to outgoing messages can be monitored and measured.

Value Creation –

Enterprise marketing actually adds something of significant value to the business as an entity. As it evolves, it will continue to achieve greater integration with a companies business processes. Think of it this way, a company that has a solid and well integrated enterprise marketing platform will sell for more than one that doesn't.

Responsiveness –

The turn around time on customer and community feedback can range from one-to-one to days, weeks or months, depending on the companies strategy. The more immediate response is particularly powerful when gauging a marketing effort and making adjustments based on historical trends and incoming data. Put simply, the wait time between strategy adjustments is significantly reduced. This allows for quicker synchronization with the real-time sentiment of your target market.

Increasing granularity –

Every year enterprise marketing platforms and their upgrades are able to produce a better defined picture of trends, motivations and statistics. Armed with this knowledge, marketers can not only address their audiences with a clearer message, they can transfer this understanding to product development.

Authenticity –

Better knowledge of your audience, due to increased granularity, targeting and responsiveness means that you don't have to pretend to know your audience, you will actually have hard data to back up your assumptions about them. This translates into great branding because real identification with the customer commonly translates into loyalty and evangelism.

Even one of these factors could create a sea change in marketing, but what is happening is that in addition to 7 significant advantages, we are also seeing increased communication and integration between business components. Coupled with economic pressures that put a massive focus on value and ROI, we can be said to be experiencing a revolution in business practices.

Employing Enterprise marketing is less a matter of deciding to use a given set of tools and more of acknowledging that it is part of the new business climate. The choice you have available to you is not whether to choose a given tool or even how to use it. The first decision is how aware you want to be of these changes and whether you want to navigate them or become the victim of those of your competitors who have.

Of course, the gravity of the situation really depends on the nature of your business as well as your future goals. If you are OK with selling lemonade on your street only and don't plan to develop systems to expand and scale out, it's unlikely recent technology and media changes will affect you.

5 8 Key Social Media Metrics and Their Actionable Responses

1) Monitor the opinions of a target demographic and online locations where a positive opinion is expressed. Natural language processing and filters can determine the key points of satisfaction as well as the various product use cases that lead to a pleased customer Online locations where negative sentiment predominates can also be identified and a more aggressive problem resolution effort can be undertaken there. This can result in pre-empting a viral explosion of ill will toward your organization.

Action:

Collect the differentiators that emerge from positive sentiment, the things your customers like most about your product and work to develop products and services more along those lines. For negative sentiment, directly address and resolve valid concerns and the individuals who have the most influence.

2) Identify cases where negative sentiment is turning into a PR crisis.

Action:

Effective social media monitoring will be able to identify key influencers before too much damage is done. This will allow you to approach them with solutions long before the horses have bolted from the barn.

   3) Identify individuals, blogs and web applications that hold the most influence over your brand.

Action:

Web community efforts in the areas identified as having the most influence. Speak to them on the terms identified by your monitoring as important to them.

   4) Keeping real-time tabs on the development of opinion and sentiment, particularly in relation to new products and services as they are released.

Action:

Not having to wait for consumer feedback means that updates, customer service and future development will be more immediately accessible. This shorter wait time between release and feedback leads to quicker issue resolution and new product development.

   5) Measure how your brand, advertising efforts, products and services play out in relation to time of day, and geo-location.

Action:

Adjust and modify products and services to specific geographies. Release your messages and ad campaigns at the time of day when most of your target customers are receptive.

   6) Determine which media types and platform protocols (Video, Short message, podcast etc) have the greatest success rate.

Action:

Focus your efforts on the media and channels that deliver the most ROI. Modify efforts in media and channels that under deliver. For example, you may learn that your video campaign, while entertaining, doesn't generate qualified leads. You may then have to focus on providing product specific and industry related video content.

   7) Monitor competitors.

Action:

Examine and emulate their success factors in areas that you can. Learn more about the sentiment of customers you would like to acquire from your competition.

8) Research the industry.

Action:

Learning about the industry in general is made possible by internet content that is more parse able along with natural language processing. This allows you to rapidly identify areas of growth, gaps and places where the market is saturated.

6 The Nine Step Enterprise And Social Media Marketing Work Flow

Create a communications strategy –

Overall, an organization must determine what its communications strategy will be. Different products will require different approaches. A soft drink, for example is less about customer complaints and trouble shooting and more about fun, excitement and contests. A technical product, like a webhost for example will be using their presence to answer questions, promote services and pre-empt major difficulties. There should be an overall theme and purpose to one's social media marketing strategy. Large organizations have more than one presence, each tuned to a different purpose.

Dell, for example has a presence for each product line as well as overall accounts that deliver news and information on new technologies along with how Dell powers them.

See a List of Dell's Social Media Presence Here

– Define message –

Before a social media and/or interactive internet marketing campaign is begun, it is necessary to define exactly what kind of message is needed. Some messages may be very simple and, like traditional media, occur redundantly over pre-scheduled times. More advanced messages can span a period of months and involve more detailed content, interaction and media.

Many companies struggle with the concept that Internet marketing is much more than advertising, it has a wide range of tools available to it and can become much more immersive than ads that blast out to recipients. Optimized social media marketing consists of a means by which data is being collected from the target audience at the very same time that it is being communicated with.

– Define tools, media and channels –

Once a communication strategy is defined, the required tools to make this vision will start to make themselves apparent. At this point, the company doing promotional work can map out the actual resources that will be required. Depending on the complexity of the effort, this is the point at which an enterprise marketing solution can be explored. Resources that may be required include, video shooting and editing, coding/scripting, design, Ajax, Flash, copy writing and analytics.

– Refine message to match tools, media and channels –

Once the tool set is collected or hired out, you'll find that the message will have to be shaped to fit into the container defined by the platform being targeted. That is, if you feel that your audience only has patience for 10 minute videos, you're idea of a 30 minute infomercial or seminar may be adjusted to a series of shorter lessons or tutorials, particularly when factoring in the possibility that you may have to pivot your content based upon viewer feedback.

Messaging will also have to be adjusted in the event that you'd like a single message from one platform to reach a variety of sites. In this case, creating a media that meets the lowest common technical denominator is required.

– Define schedule –

Your message may or may depend on redundancy, serialization (A regular schedule), Community response or the times of day that most of your target audience is online. This needs to be defined and measured for affordability in terms of the media that will have to be produced.

Broadcast –

Once prepared for content and format and schedule, the message can be broadcasted.

If the above steps are prepared correctly and a service/platform for sending information is intelligently selected, this should be a simple step. Otherwise, you can find yourself submitting things manually and consuming valuable time that should be devoted to analysis and modification.

Collect Data –

Data collection can be as simple as visiting your social network accounts and checking for responses, or as complex as gathering this data via a third party service provider. Information collected this way can be interpreted by their interface or sent to your own business intelligence system.

Analyze data – In terms of marketing –

The data returned is then examined for trends and insights into the market and the response to your communication efforts. Many products immediately produce graphs that illustrate the basics, like click-throughs, source and number of times a given message has been resent. Beyond this, services vary as to how much detail and tracking is included with the service.

Analyze data – In terms of business processes –

Analyzing the same data from this perspective can reveal redundancies, inefficiencies, waste and un-utilized features/services that can eventually be phased out as a cost savings measure.

Modify processes and marketing strategies -

Communications responses and customer feed back can then be studied for how it applies to product design and other processes that face the customer. Once communications feedback is understood, processes can strategies can be modified, stopped, initiated or expanded upon.

Rinse and Repeat –

Once an updated or new strategy is created, it is again broadcasted thus repeating the cycle of creation, broadcast and improvement. Optimally, all business processes are linked to a more comprehensive communication with the consumer and the vehicle of a business is propelled forward by a closer, more accurate and more granular link to the people that they serve.

Again, this is not just social media marketing, it is using what is essentially a distributed communications platform and networked database that is accessible via a wide range of hardware (PC, mobile, gaming device) to deliver more business value, greater customer satisfaction and involvement. Shifting the focus to the total phenomenon of the Internet rather than to a particular web application, format, media type or moniker Du Jour, will help to maintain focus on this force as an evolving business tool rather than an erratically defined techno-mantra.

7 Linking Enterprise Marketing To Internal Business Processes

As mentioned and explained in previous chapters, online marketing via social media and other internet media is on a collision course with business intelligence. This in only natural because Social Media and Enterprise Marketing both need to accumulate and broadcast a large amount of data. Since business intelligence is essentially the analysis of data in order to reveal key business insights, the two are naturally complimentary, and have already become inextricably linked in a symbiotic two way flow of information analysis and communication.

Already, larger companies with well established and more complex business intelligence systems are piping communications data and audience feedback into their systems. Companies like SAP, Oracle and IBM are adding increasingly comprehensive social media metrics to their products. This is great for very large organizations with large budgets and if you have this kind of money, these solutions are well worth a look. On the other hand given that this area is so rapidly developing, it might be unwise to invest heavily in a solution tailored to what may turn out to be an erroneous vision of future internet development.

The sector is mature yet it is important to examine the potential of distributed social interaction as a tool for business development first. Each Social Media Marketing/Enterprise Marketing solution provider has a different approach to mapping the data value of online interaction to business processes, and to a different degree of depth. The differences across companies can be driven by the target cost of the product or the philosophy of the service provider with regards to how internet activity should be interpreted and acted upon. In addition, the needs of the market have a say in what kind of products are created.

Since many of these products end users are still understanding the technology, evaluating their needs and deciding on budget, the sweet spot for service providers is still in flux. In addition, the newness and rapid growth of these technologies makes for a particularly dynamic market and product selection. Let's take a look at three of the bigger vendors and see how their approach to to mapping social media to business intelligence varies.

SAP/Jive –

Rather than handling social media on their own. Jive has produced a module for acquiring and feeding social media data into SAP business objects. One thing this business arrangement points out is that SAP seems to have come to the conclusion that the maintaining an effective internet presence is complex enough to warrant a partnership with another organization rather than the creation of a new segment of the organization. Using their plug-in architecture, customers can use their existing investment in business intelligence and enhance its capabilities by collecting and interpreting distributed communications.

This is a sensible approach in that expertise is regulated to a separate organization with the agility and flexibility to keep up with the rapid changes in this arena. While this looks to be a highly effective solution, if does require SAP and the requisite costs and technical skills. Beyond that, such a solution may be overkill for smaller businesses.

Also, the modular approach, where satellite companies provide solutions for partner companies only works well if one of the companies has a large ecosystem of customers. Otherwise, purchasing a core system and module can run you into big problems if the company responsible for the core architecture runs into business issues.

IBM –

IBM is working with SPSS, a company that they own, to focus on the analytics of internet interaction data. The support literature seems to focus on the analysis aspect, once interaction data has been collected. Tools and strategy are not stressed as part of the solution. Since data analysis and public relations are fully unique and disparate disciplines, it makes sense for companies providing the top end of the spectrum to not even attempt to know about something that requires a completely different set of resources. The assumption is that companies paying high fees for IT will also be paying for independently competent communication strategy solutions.

The SAP jive approach hints at an integration between communication and analytics, but from a PR solution/Marketing perspective, its a far cry from a fully developed strategy. The gist of their emphasis on communication focus is to illustrate that their tools are useable and understandable by PR/Marketing professionals.

SAS –

Being more oriented toward statistical analysis than business processes, SAS is in a position to create their own social media analytics offering rather that to partner with a third party. The obvious advantage is that SAS knows its own products and as a customer, you are not reliant on the ability of a large and third party company being able to communicate with each other. Perhaps one significant disadvantage is that while SAS will be able to crunch numbers flawlessly, they will most likely be far less adept at handling the softer communication related skill set, or to be able to write code and architecture to that aspect.

A third party module creator, on the other hand may be writing their software specifically from a communications facilitation perspective and is likely to have such experts on staff. Comparing the online resource library of both companies provides a clue. SAS has articles and white papers focused on the statistical analysis and information available from social data whereas Jive has quite a few articles and white papers on online community building strategies.

Oracle –

At present, the verdict on Oracles solutions tends to be that they are taking more of a snap on widget approach than anything comprehensive. Some industry commentators have even concluded that this reflects a more conservative wait and see approach that may result in them not only falling behind in this sector but also doing a bit of damage to themselves by not showing the foresight to get more fully engaged in mapping social media to business processes. Each of these solutions certainly has room for improvement and increased integration between social data and business strategy.

There is a huge gap between marketing message creation and data analysis but it is a space begging to be filled. The soft arts of personal communication have always been the antithesis of logic models, but social media has appeared as a node between the two extremes, and companies on both sides of the gap are now working hard to fill that space. Part of this will consist of developing communications and messaging that is always in a state that can be tracked, parsed, stored and retrieved, while at the same time having the immediacy of real-time relevance and authenticity.

There are two locations in the chain that represent significant gaps, and one area (social media) that is developing rapidly, with major players (Twitter, Facebook etc) who's evolving function sets will create interconnections between themselves. This hoped for ideal is a complete link between end user/customer and product creation/business processes on a one to one basis. This is a long way off of course, but ironically, a lot of this development will come from the recession driven need to cut costs. It can be argued that without the recession, all ends of this spectrum would be content to continue to do business using familiar, albeit financially wasteful ways.

Worse still, they may have continued or reactivated the kind of dot com era ebullience and flash & feature rich bloat and led to many overvalued start ups and their well known fate. Today, in this climate, forward steps are rarely taken unless management is still well within reach of displayable ROI. This change will result in smarter spending and more sustainable, even and profitable growth in the long term.

8   7 Social Media Metrics That Drive Industry Development

Types of data from the social internet:

Consumer trends –

Mining review sites and comparing the number of comments shown for a given type of products across several product creators can reveal significant data on how frequently a product is purchased as compared to similar products from another company. There are already sites that aggregate and collect comments, like Disqus which also have an API that allows for parsing through comments to find keywords and specific types of comments.

Consumer Opinions –

Similar to the above, but for sites that have a specific consumer orientation as well as specific methods of inputting and recording consumer data.

Ratings –

If only interested in numerical values, this information can be taken out and used as a very concise summary of sentiment.

Desires for improvements –

Review sites comments can often have in their comments expressed wished for improvements that can be made. This allows marketers to get a more realistic evaluation of what is wanted by the target group.

Level of Evangelism –

Some people recommend a product, while others evangelize it. The converse is also true in cases where the product or service is considered to be very poor.

Location and Density of Communities –

Those who speak about a given product may be primarily located at a single web site or spread out across several. Knowing the distribution pattern of a product type's consumer will help to identify the areas where greater influence can be projected.

Degree of involvement in the product – Some products may have several small reviews. Others may have a smaller number of very detailed information on the product. Both types of engagement reveal something key about consumer behavior with regards to it.

Actionable steps on this information include, targeting areas with the greatest social influence, engaging specific users who provide valuable feedback, reaching out to bloggers of influence with promotions and incentives, altering products to suit stated needs and emulating the success factors of highly populated communities in order to create one around your product that you can manage yourself.

With the social internet in its basic stages, many companies are still defining their Social Media interaction to be little more than creating a Facebook page on the product. As the data from online communities becomes more freely available, it can be parsed more easily. As with OpenID, Facebook Login and Twitter Login, there will emerge standardized formats for inputting interaction data with regard to opinions and ratings. As this happens, the coding of applications designed to aggregate and process this information will become easier to both write and modularize, again, all to the end of creating significant ROI over traditional yet costly and poorly targeted traditional market research.

9 Test The Social Media/Enterprise Marketing Waters For Free

To get started with Enterprise Marketing, take a look at some of the free online tools that can provide insight into activity related to one or more of your internet presences. Below is a table that lists some free sights that provide these metrics. What you need to be aware of is that these applications will only provide a glimpse of the kind of analytics that are available. What you need to ask yourself when using these free services is whether this information and extensions on this information will be useful. Your answer will most likely be 'Yes'. Getting referenced, forwarded or retweeted by someone can be a big boost to an organization. Automating and scaling messages that spread virally can represent huge cost savings and marketing ROI. As sites such as Twitter, Facebook and Youtube continue to add features, they will accumulate ever vaster amounts of demographic data and also continue to find ways of making this data available to marketers in an ethical transparent manner. The latter is a matter of working out technical and perception bugs but this is an infrastructure that can be built.

Here are some examples and what they provide:

Twitalyzer

http://www.twitalyzer.com/

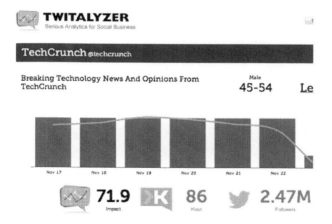

A nice interactive UI rich set of analytics for your Twitter presence, allows for integration with Google analytics, it is free but more complete analytics start at $9.99/month.

Klout

This application examines your Twitter account and provides a series of metrics, including feedback on how influential you are. This is useful when testing strategies for obtaining recognition as an authority in your area. Also free.

Hubspot

A comprehensive suite of social media broadcasting and analytics and marketing automation.

Measure the Business Value of Social Media

Does Facebook really work for business? How much time should you be spending on Twitter? Is Google+ something you need to consider? Until recently, the impact of social media has been notoriously hard to measure. With HubSpot, you can finally start reporting on the ROI of social media.

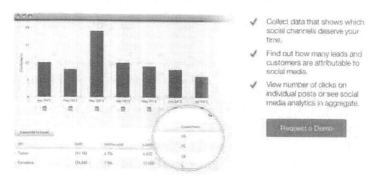

✓ Collect data that shows which social channels deserve your time.

✓ Find out how many leads and customers are attributable to social media.

✓ View number of clicks on individual posts or see social media analytics in aggregate.

Request a Demo

Compose a message

HootSuite

Another well rounded solution. Analytics, broadcasting and marketing automation.

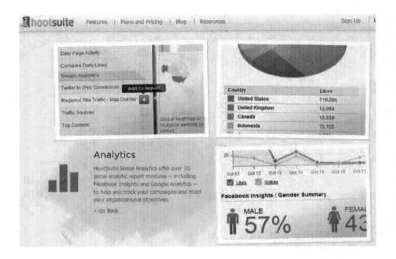

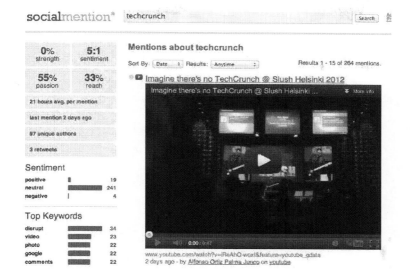

Socialmention.com pours over the web and examines your metrics across the internet. Considering the scope of its search, the amount of information you get from this free service is quite impressive.

Facebook analytics, providing stats on your applications, ad campaigns and audience demographics. Webtrends also provides a number of other applications that track a variety of data sources other than Facebook. What you may find from companies like this, is that each of the products can be purchased individually. This is great if you have a focus in a primary area and have determined a valid need by examining free tools first, but if you are not careful, you may end up with the same daily routine that you'd have if you were to use the free web sites. That is, bouncing around from screen to screen, trying to aggregate various collections of insight into something actionable.

Ubervu.com

Ubervu is similar to socialmention.com in that is examines the internet presence of a site of keyword. It tends to pull from sources with an API, so the data may be more reliable, but also with a more limited set of sources.

Ping has merged with Seesmic, which has been acquired by HootSuite. This has resulted in a powerful set of tools which allow for both social media broadcasting and analytics. The Seesmic Ping Components are Shown Below.

Features

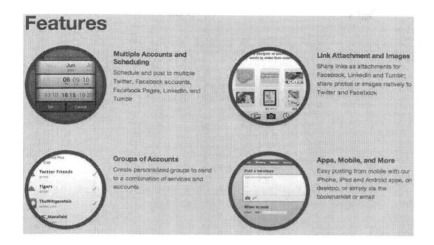

Multiple Accounts and Scheduling
Schedule and post to multiple Twitter, Facebook accounts, Facebook Pages, LinkedIn, and Tumblr

Link Attachment and Images
Share links as attachments for Facebook, LinkedIn and Tumblr; share photos or images natively to Twitter and Facebook

Groups of Accounts
Create personalized groups to send to a combination of services and accounts

Apps, Mobile, and More
Easy posting from mobile with our iPhone, iPad and Android apps, on desktop, or simply via the bookmarklet or email

While most of these examples are Twitter specific, the same services exist for Youtube, Google, Facebook and any of the other major social networks out there. There are too many others to mention, and by the time you read this, some may have shut down while others may have started up, that's the nature of the Internet. You should go to Google and search for Social Media analytics or Social Media measurement and see what comes up. Some applications will be more robust than others, some can take awhile to compile your stats. This is the price of a free service. In addition, these tools can be subject to the whims of the platform, their API limits or privacy issues.

Take a couple of days to shop through these tools and create a table that lists the service, URL, functionality, stability/speed and finally in a separate column check whether the tool has a potential business use for you. As you learn about what's out there, you'll be able to define your requirements when shopping for a more complete solution. ...And you will need a complete solution, bouncing around between all of these web interfaces, can be extremely time consuming, tedious and will eventually lead to a lack of follow up.

The next section reveals a minimum of what you should be expecting and asking for when considering giving your business to a dedicated, more comprehensive and expensive social media/enterprise marketing service provider. Whenever a new business sector opens up, there is a glut of companies, consultants and shysters who are more adept at spinning buzzwords than actually creating value. It is absolutely essential that you find out for yourself what is available for free before you take a strangers word on what a given service or feature should cost. You shouldn't be paying for whiz bang graphics, UI and deft programming hackery, but real measurable business value.

Things will eventually shake out to the point where the gap between customer knowledge and consultant hype narrows, but unfortunately, most of us are in the position of having to decide and implement now. Many of these available tools also have their own API, so you or your tech-literate colleagues can roll your own solution if you like.

In the process you'll learn a great deal about how such systems work, the value they can provide and the overall landscape of this sector. Be warned though that you'll have to deal with API limits, scaling issues from the data source, and additional equipment/staff purchases. In fact, as this art/science evolves you'll eventually need to open up a dedicated department, probably sooner than later. Finally, if Twitalizer for example, has it's own API, that's great but remember that Twitalyzer depends on the Twitter API. This means a chain of dependencies.

At this point, outsourcing this work to another service provider starts to make sense. Sure, they are also subject to API limits, privacy concerns and scaling issues, but because of their volume and history in the market, they've been able to forge much more stable relationships with Twitter, Facebook, Google, Youtube etc, along with the fatter data pipe that this kind of relationship includes. Also keep in mind that the large social media platforms have something to gain by seeing social media enterprise/marketing service providers prove ROI. Smaller, single proprietor outfits generally tend to tax resources and increase exposure to privacy and security issues until they reach a certain size. Finally, time spent on rolling your own social media/internet analytics package is time better spent on your core business.

In effect, an examination of these free services is absolutely in order for the insight it provides into the emerging art and science of enterprise marketing. This kind of research arms you with the knowledge necessary to evaluate your needs against what is possible via the analysis of internet data. Next we'll take a look at how you should shop for a paid service provider, what to look for, what to expect and how to use the data and reports that you'll be receiving.

10 Available Solutions and 17 Essential Questions to ask a potential vendor

Company	Free trial	Social media Analytics	Social media Broadcasting	Social media Monitoring	Social media Campaign Management	Analyze Business and Social media Data For Insight	Natural Language Processing
ATTENITY		*		*		Complete analytics suite	*
ALTERIAN	You Click Here	*	*	*	*	Complete analytics suite	
SiteCatalyst. _Extremely comprehensive covers Social media, CRM and Business Intelligence		*	*	*	*	Complete analytics suite	
cymfony		*		*		Insight Into Campaign Control and Strategies	*

If you've taken the suggestion in the previous chapter and had a look around at some of the free offerings, you'll be able to see that there are certain classes of business value that emerge as well as certain kinds of requirements that one should look for. As with any set of products, what is available is on a spectrum along with corresponding price differences.

The business value that is provided by even the free accounts should be visible at this point. Insight into audience behavior, their concerns, how your name is playing out, response to a sample of your messaging to name a few. You've probably also run into some of the limitations that these free services provide. Namely, speed, reliability and depth. You may in fact still be waiting for one of more of the sights you went to to finish crunching your stats. Such is the nature of a free web-based service and one or two such experiences should make it clear that this is no way to do business. At this point the choice is to either roll your own or step up and invest in a more reliable product and service.

Making your own will be prohibitive for most people, so we'll look at making a purchase and the research required to do so wisely. The survey of free services you have given you insight into what particular feature you can expect, but not necessarily the fundamental characteristics behind a given feature set. So let's clarify. Below is a list of characteristics that will cost more in proportion to an increase in quality and quantity. What to look for:

Granularity – How fine is that data? It is possible to drill down to a single visitor, tweet, Facebook update or account? Weigh the offering against what you really need right now.

Depth – How deep does the data go? How many relationships can it traverse. Heavy business intelligence products can go all over the place, many times analyzing data automatically, finding relationships that you've never thought of exploring. An SME may only need a subset of this depth, so don't get talked into buying more scope than you need.

Historical data – Extended use of free online analytics will eventually reveal that historical data is often flushed. These smaller organizations can hardly afford to keep legacy data on the shelves if it is recalled only a fraction of the time. Obviously, the more you pay, the more history you'll get, and with greater granularity. That having been said, you may have defined your marketing strategy to be responsive to only a couple of years, or a couple of months. Marketing in a developing country is a perfect example, there simply isn't enough reliable historical data in many locations.

UI – User interface can be de-emphasized as an obvious angle for a salesperson to take, but it cannot be discounted as completely useless. Good UI makes powerful insight not only rapidly visible, but rapidly actionable. In a real time environment, this is crucial. The question you should ask yourself when shopping then isn't 'How jelly like are the buttons?' but 'How quickly can I get from a set of key data/statistics to generating a new message to a given target audience?' When comparing products, articulate this question to the sales person and measure the time it takes to get a response. In fact, this information should not have to be asked for, the sales literature or sales person should be honing in on and demonstrating on this sales point ASAP.

Modularity – Social Media/Enterprise Marketing companies run a whole spectrum between what are essentially PR companies to full blown IT shops with varying combinations of marketing/IT expertise thrown in. You need to decide which mix suits you best. As you approach more IT focused providers, you'll need to inquire as to how separable the components of a given solution are. That is, can the different parts be combined in different ways to reveal different insights?

Data can be viewed and processed in an infinite number of ways, how much freedom do you have to isolate views and combine them in ways that more accurately model your own organization? Again, focus on modularity to the degree that it meets your needs, not to the extent that it meets some abstract concept of perfection.

Ability to tie to other business components – Can these internet marketing analytics be fed into a large business intelligence component, and with how much ease? This is like attaching the tire to the body of a car. If the data cannot be piped in directly to your business intelligence, it will be up to you to do the interpretation and data re-entry into your database, spreadsheet or other BI warehouse.

51

This would be like racing down the track while physically holding the tire out with your own two hands. For a small company, it might seem like excess to have all such units tied together, but the price of all these services is coming down rapidly, so make sure you are not harboring assumptions that were made a year ago.

Ability for automation – Can actionable data and statistics be scripted to increase, decrease, stop or start a particular messaging channel in response to pre-set values? This is quite advanced, but the obvious benefit is that real time response does not have to rely on constant human interaction. This frees up time for strategizing from a longer perspective. For global organizations, this can be a key feature, the ability to tune a message for an overseas market while headquarters is sound asleep. Response from global markets is accelerated.

Ability to respond – Some analytics services may not even offer the ability to respond, but may be focused solely on providing data and reports. This may be all you need. If so, there is no point in paying for more.

Granularity of response – Can your responses to reporting consist of one message to all platforms, or different messages to different platforms,demographics, geo-locations, devices, etc.?

Portability of data – Can the data your activity generates be transferred to another platform? You may outgrow your current service, or find that you are not using some features that push up the cost, requiring you to downgrade. In either case, you'll need a way for that data to get from point a to point b, otherwise you'll lose historical information.

Ownership of the data – This issue has not come up in a big way yet, but it is conceivable that if Facebook can claim ownership of a person's personal data, perhaps a social media/Enterprise marketing company may claim that while they don't own what is said about you on some blog, they do have ownership rights of the stats and analysis that their algorithms produce. This is a point worth considering, particularly if historical data is important to you. If you decide to cancel their service, you may find that you are only entitled to the raw, un-parsed and un-compiled data, essentially a gargantuan unsorted text file. Something to think about. This is why you should think of data portability not in terms of an exit from the service, but in terms of being able to export data at any time, in a useable format, without the assistance of their staff.

Search capabilities – Search is an essential component of any of these systems. It is what allows you to access the power of the analytics in its complete form. You need to look for a wide range of filtering capabilities such as time, location, platforms and the ability to exclude certain items. In effect, search should be as configurable as you need it to be.

Spam management – Blogs, messaging systems and forums are all subject to spam and content that is clearly not relevant to your needs. Any system you are looking at should be able to filter out this data before it enters your database and business intelligence system.

Alert functionality – Rather than wait until you search for it to realize that you are now in a full blown PR crisis, it would be better to have some configurable alert functionality to that you will be alerted when a particular number has been reached or situation has occurred. This is not only a matter of damage control, it is also a matter of being able to capitalize on positive responses from a given channel as soon as possible so that you can feed positive momentum.

File and reports management – As you continue to use a given system, you'll quickly have a mass of reports, data and suggestions. What is the storage system for these items and how easy plus quick is it to pull this information?

A Demo – Many service providers have a free demo that is available for you to use for a limited time or with a limited feature set. See the list below for a directory of companies, their feature set and their demo.

11 Index – 5 Pillars, Top 5 White Papers on SMBI

Social Media:

Top Social Media Tools of 2012

Business Intelligence:

8 Business Analytics Essentials

CRM:

The New Rules of Relationship Management

Marketing:

Marketing with Big Data to Increase ROI

Internal Processes:

ERP as a Living System

12 About the author

This paper is provided by CIOWhitePapers, a leading source of technical white papers on topics as diverse as Business Intelligence, Social Media Marketing, Big Data, Cloud Computing and Emerging Marketing Technologies. CIOWhitePapers works with industry leaders such as Oracle, IBM, Google, Forrester Consulting, Wildfire, Hootsuite and a wide variety of drivers in internet infrastructure, content and commerce. Together, they provide exclusive industry news, trends and updates for executive decision makers in a wide variety of information related industries.

Printed in Great Britain
by Amazon.co.uk, Ltd.,
Marston Gate.